MW00655159

EXPERIENCING THE FATHER'S LOVE

LEARNING TO LIVE AS SONS AND DAUGHTERS OF OUR HEAVENLY FATHER

OS HILLMAN

Printed in the United States of America

Aslan Group Publishing, 475 Tribble Gap Road, Ste 110, Cumming, Georgia 30040 USA

www.marketplaceleaders.org

ISBN 978-0-578-04447-7

"I will be a Father to you, And you shall be My sons and daughters," says the Lord Almighty. –2 Corinthians 6:18

And because you are sons, God has sent forth the Spirit of His Son into your hearts, crying out, "Abba, Father!" Therefore you are no longer a slave but a son, and if a son, then an heir of God through Christ. –Galatians 4:6, 7

To my daughter, Charis Rebecca
I love you.

Experiencing the Father's Love

Learning to Live as Sons and Daughters of Our Heavenly Father

CHAPTER ONE

When God Thinks of You, Love Swells in his Heart

The Lord your God in your midst, the Mighty One, will save; He will rejoice over you with gladness, He will quiet you with His love, He will rejoice over you with singing (Zeph. 3:17).

"When God thinks of you, love swells in his heart." I can imagine the thoughts going through your mind as you reflect on that statement. For many of us, this idea is hard to accept. Do you really believe God loves you, even delights in you? If you are a follower of Christ you will probably give me the politically correct answer and say, "Yes. I believe He does." However, most of us will respond to that statement perhaps with a "Well, yes, but...". It is hard for us to believe God loves us without adding a "but" after the statement. The very statement challenges our theology about God. Many of us associate the nature of God with holiness, judgment, and righteousness. Our first cognitive association with that statement will be based on beliefs and conclusions we have formed from our individual life experiences. The opening verse from Zephaniah reveals the true heart of God toward us. He rejoices over us with gladness, love, and singing! The psalmist says "How precious also are Your thoughts to me, O God! How great is the sum of them!"[1]

I'll be honest with you. When I first heard that opening statement, I found it hard to grasp. "Yeah, I believe that God loves me if I have been good and not sinned." Or, maybe I might think, "Yeah, I guess I can believe that sometimes." Or, "Well, you don't know how much I've failed God." That one statement can reveal how much we've all been impacted by shame and our need to perform to gain love.

In my own experience, deep down I didn't really believe God loved me without conditions. Part of me required me to earn that love. Our actions often determine what we really believe about God, don't they? Our ability to see God as an unconditionally loving Heavenly Father is formed by many factors—our earthly father, the type of parenting we received growing up, and the wounds we received as a child. The type of church experience we've had also impacts our beliefs. These factors determine whether our view of God is rooted in love as opposed to fear, performance, shame or legalism.

If I were to do a survey of the average Christian and ask why God created man, my guess is the answers would be as follows:

- To worship God.
- To evangelize the whole world.
- To work on His behalf.

I doubt the first answer would be to have friendship and intimacy with God Himself. It simply is not our first line of thinking. We have been trained to worship, to fulfill the great commission, and to work for Him. Don't get me wrong, all of this is important. However, by missing the core reason for His creating you and me, we miss the core motivation for what we do. Our Christian life becomes defined by what we do and how well we do it, instead of how well we know the Creator and His motivation for creating us in the first place. Activity should come as a result of the relationship, not the other way around.

Winning the lost and impacting the world is the fruit of the relationship Jesus spoke of in John 15 when He said we could do nothing without abiding in the Vine. The church's failure to emphasize our need for intimacy with the Father is exemplified by the number of evangelism strategies and programs designed to win the lost as compared to those designed to help us understand and experience the love of God in our own lives. True transformation only comes when we experience the deep level of love from our Father in a vulnerability that transfers to others. Jesus said, "You will know my disciples by the love they have for one another." The focus is on knowing versus doing.

When Jesus died, He destroyed the performance model of obeying the 10 commandments to be acceptable to God. Up until Jesus, people were very much defined by their performance measured against the law. He changed the rules and said, "Accepting Me alone is what makes you acceptable."

GOD AS OUR FATHER

In Psalms it says, "When my father and my mother forsake me, then the Lord will take care of me" (Psalm 27:10). You are the helper of the fatherless" (Psalm 10:14).

To truly believe we are loved by God and can experience that love, we must overcome a number of personal hurdles. Many of us must overcome the dysfunctional family systems we were brought up in. Our earthly fathers may have taught us that a Heavenly Father could be a dictator, a rejecter of his own offspring, a sexual abuser, a boot camp sergeant, or a traffic cop. These attributes have been the only characteristics of earthly fathers that many people have known. So, to relate to a Heavenly Father as unconditionally loving requires a miracle of sorts. There must be a time of healing from such wounds in order to experience God at a deeply personal love level. This often requires an intentional process of counseling or personal ministry. We must replace what we experienced with what we know the truth to be—that we are loveable and that our Heavenly Father loves us.

I lost my dad when I was fourteen years old to an airplane crash. The plane totally burned and there was no body, so I did not get to see my dad in a casket. I experienced some fantasies related to his death in which I thought I saw him in his car around town. This was not true, but because I never saw him dead, I thought that maybe he was not actually dead. It was not until a counseling session in my mid-fifties that I realized for the first time that I had never adequately grieved the loss of my dad. I was forced to grow up sooner than I should have as a fourteen year old and the only son in the family. I also had not recognized how his death greatly affected my inability to relate to the love of the Father in my own life. Subconsciously I believed I was abandoned by my father, so in essence, my Heavenly Father also abandoned me. It was difficult for me to relate to my Heavenly Father at a heart level. This led to putting a shell around my heart and creating a wall that was impenetrable by others who wanted to get close as a defense mechanism to avoid being hurt again. This was all done at a subconscious level.

The Father as Our Protector

> *"Look at the birds of the air. Consider the lilies in the field. Are you not much more valuable to your true Father than they?" (Matthew 6:26, 28).*

The truth is that most humans, just like Adam and Eve, believe God is holding out on them. We don't really believe God's true nature is love. Suppose you are a brand new recruit in the army and your assignment in Afghanistan is to cross a field that is loaded with mines. A ten year veteran soldier scout is with you and he has learned how the enemy places mines in the fields so that you cannot see them. However, your experienced scout knows how they hide them and has learned to recognize the signs of where the mines are located. Are you going to ignore his advice? I don't know about you, but I would stay as close to that person as I could. I would stay right behind him the whole way. His directions to me would preserve my life. I would be stupid not to rely on his guidance through that field. God is the same way. He wants to protect us from the minefields of life. However, many of us simply do not believe God has our best interest in mind. We believe He is going to place limits upon us that will prevent us from doing what we really want to do.

When we live under a belief that God loves us we also understand what it means to live under God's authority, knowing His nature is always love towards us no matter how it might appear to our limited understanding. We understand that God gives us freedoms and boundaries for our benefit, not to put limits on our lives.

Understanding Our 7 Needs

God created man to have seven needs as human beings. They include the following:

1. Dignity
2. Authority
3. Blessing & Provision
4. Security
5. Purpose & Meaning
6. Freedom & Boundary
7. Intimate Love & Companionship[2]

These needs are not listed categorically in Genesis 1 and 2, but are implied in many different ways as you read through these two chapters. It is important for us to realize God created mankind with these seven needs because unless we understand this we do not understand why we are tempted to meet our needs outside God's design. Understanding this foundation will help us understand how we are to receive from God in appropriate ways and how we are often motivated to receive by meeting our own needs outside God's order.

We are all tempted to gain things in life outside the parameters of God's intended plan. One of the primary strategies that Satan uses in our lives is to manipulate outcomes outside God's intended plan. The more we begin to meet our own needs in our own way the more we open ourselves up to entry points where Satan begins to establish territory in our lives. Over time a stronghold is developed which the apostle Paul describes as follows: "For though we walk in the flesh, we do not war according to the flesh. For the weapons of our warfare are not carnal but mighty in God for pulling down strongholds, casting down arguments and every high thing that exalts itself against the knowledge of God, bringing every thought into captivity to the obedience of

Christ, and being ready to punish all disobedience when your obedience is fulfilled" (2 Cor 10:3-6). Notice some key thoughts expressed in this very important passage.

- Strongholds are a *belief system* that entices us to argue against the knowledge of God.
- It is a *thought or idea* that is not rooted in God which motivates us to meet our own needs.
- It is a form of *disobedience* to the ways of God.

When Jesus was baptized and fasted and prayed for forty days, Satan came to him and tried to convince Him to meet His needs outside God's design and purposes. Satan tried to appeal to Jesus by actually misquoting scripture to Him. "Then Jesus was led up by the Spirit into the wilderness to be tempted by the devil. And when He had fasted forty days and forty nights, afterward He was hungry. Now when the tempter came to Him, he said, "If You are the Son of God, command that these stones become bread.' But He answered and said, 'It is written, 'Man shall not live by bread alone, but by every word that proceeds from the mouth of God.'" Then the devil took Him up into the holy city, set Him on the pinnacle of the temple, and said to Him, 'If You are the Son of God, throw Yourself down. For it is written:

He shall give His angels charge over you' and, in their hands they shall bear you up, lest you dash your foot against a stone'" (Matt 4:1-6).

Jesus was physically hungry. His need was for food. But Jesus knew that what God wanted Him to receive at that time was not physical food, but spiritual food. *He refused to receive what He knew He was not to receive at that time.* Satan tried to convince him to refocus His attention on His physical need, not His spiritual need. Satan was trying to change Jesus' belief system and what to believe about meeting His needs.

Sometimes a stronghold can develop as a natural defense mechanism to being hurt by another person such as a parent, sibling or even an accident. If you were abused when you were young you will tend to have built-in defenses to avoid being hurt again. However, all spiritual strongholds in our lives develop when we begin to focus on meeting a need in our lives outside God's intended way. It tempts us to believe a lie about the nature of our Heavenly Father. It happens in a myriad of ways:

- A wife desires to feel better about herself by going out and meeting that emotional need through a shopping spree at the mall.

- A business owner uses manipulation and control to motivate his employees to greater performance because of his fear of failure rather than seeking God for strategy on how to be successful.
- A man has an overwhelming need for sex so he visits pornographic websites rather than developing intimacy with his God and his wife that can meet his emotional and physical needs.
- A teenage boy gets involved in drugs to mask the emotional pain of rejection from a father or mother.
- A teenage girl has a baby out of wedlock because she is longing for the love of her father but instead seeks love in the wrong places.
- A business owner commits fraud in a business because the pressures to succeed at all costs outweigh the integrity of his soul.

The stories are countless of how human beings seek to meet needs outside God the Father's intended plan. Many times the underlying motivations in our hearts are often tainted by difficult life experiences. The unresolved pain in our lives due to emotional wounds we received when we were young can tempt us to have defense mechanisms to meet our needs apart from God because we believe God has been holding out on us or we simply don't want to be hurt again. This is a plan of the enemy – to make us believe a lie about the nature of our Heavenly Father. Recognizing that this spiritual battle exists will help us better understand how to take our needs to our Heavenly Father who truly desires to meet our every need.

Today, evaluate the seven needs you have in your own life and determine if you are seeking to meet those seven needs through your Heavenly Father or you are seeking to meet them through a spiritual stronghold in your life.

CHAPTER TWO

Overcoming the Spirit of Rejection

For some of us the reason we are unable to connect with the love of the Father is due to the influence of a spirit of rejection that visits us through past generations. We must realize we are at war with unseen forces even before we were born. The apostle Paul in Ephesians 6:12 says "We wrestle not against flesh and blood, but against principalities, against powers, against the rulers of the darkness of this world, against spiritual wickedness in high places." These principalities live in the realm of the spirit and they are able to influence us beyond our conscious thought with impressions, feelings, and ideas that make us believe the feelings are ours. They are able to trigger things in us without even thinking about it. Entertaining a spirit of rejection is actually sin because we are disagreeing with what God says about us. We have no right to reject ourselves if God has accepted us. We might say to ourselves: "God, You made a mistake when You created me. I am rejected and for You to tell me that I am not rejected is a lie. So You are a liar." When we go into self-rejection, we are telling God He is a liar. It sets man as our god by declaring that who we are rests on a human who accepts us or does not accept us. In order to remove the influence of this spirit we must confess our sin and renounce it. This will allow us to begin to believe God when He says that we are truly loved.

Despite going to the cross, Jesus did not allow a spirit of rejection to make him doubt the Father's love for Him. Jesus spoke of the "prince of this world finding no place in Him" and therefore having no authority over Him. When a 'prince' has a place in us it has authority over matters in our life. Jesus had to battle His thoughts to the point of sweating blood in Gethsemane because He was living as a human being with the same temptations as us. Because He was tempted, He was able to relate to our struggles. "For in that He Himself has suffered, being tempted, He is able to aid those who are tempted."[3]

However, He did not yield to the temptation. Jesus believed He was loved, and loved Himself, which allowed Him to love others. We must do the same. We must reject the spirit of rejection and any unloving spirits designed to make us live in shame. Shame makes us feel like we are flawed whenever we fail. It isolates us as being the failure instead of our behavior being the problem. Guilt is God's method of convicting us of sin through the Holy Spirit. God never rejects us as His son or daughter. He only rejects our sin. He is always redemptive in His correction of us in an effort to maintain relationship.

Cain and Abel

The first example of a spirit of rejection operating in the Bible was in the story of Cain and Abel. Cain was a farmer and Abel was a shepherd. When Cain and Abel brought offerings to the Lord, God rejected Cain's offering. The reason was that Cain brought his offering out of duty, but Abel offered his from his heart. God judged Cain's motive and rejected his offering. However, God did not reject Cain as a person. It was here that the spirit of rejection began to influence Cain and he believed the lie that God did not love him and had rejected him.

"Abel also brought of the firstborn of his flock and of their fat. And the Lord respected Abel and his offering, but He did not respect Cain and his offering. And Cain was very angry, and his countenance fell. So the Lord said to Cain, 'Why are you angry?

And why has your countenance fallen? If you do well, will you not be accepted? And if you do not do well, sin lies at the door. And its desire is for you, but you should rule over it.'"[4]

God tried to warn Cain that what he was doing was not pleasing, but Cain believed that God was rejecting him personally, and he got angry. This led to bitterness toward God and envy and jealousy toward his brother. This root of bitterness grew to murder. God warned Cain that "sin lies at the door." Cain sinned by believing a lie about not being accepted by God. Shame (his countenance fell) tells us that WE are not acceptable; guilt says we did something wrong and need to repent, but we are still accepted by God.

You Have a Stronghold of Rejection

I was in Singapore several years ago and a woman came up to me after a teaching session on spiritual strongholds. She asked if I could meet with her and a friend after the session for lunch to discuss what I had just taught. I noticed the woman was very aggressive and would not take no for an answer. I also noticed she was about 15-20 pounds overweight. We sat down for lunch and I asked her if she could answer a question for me before I answered any of her questions. "Tell me about the relationship you have with your father." She was surprised by the question.

"Why would you want to know that?"

"Well, before I tell you, would you please tell me about that relationship."

"Oh, I have a horrible relationship with my dad. He says I will never amount to anything and that I am fat."

"I see." I turned to her and said, "You have a stronghold of rejection that has impacted you your entire life. You live to gain approval from your dad. This is why you are so aggressive and competitive. You must win at all costs because your life is rooted in performance in hopes you will gain approval from your father. You live your whole life in hopes of getting that approval someday." Although I did not tell her this, I knew the weight issue was rooted also in this. She sabotaged her weight as part of an agreement or vow. She would not actually allow herself to succeed subconsciously to prove her father was right about her. She needed to be released from her stronghold of rejection. As I shared these words she began to cry in the restaurant. "No one has ever said these words to me. However, what you are saying is true. I do live for his approval." I led this woman in a prayer of deliverance and told her she no longer needed to please her father. She was totally accepted by her Heavenly Father.

For many of us the Christian life has been more about avoiding sin, performing, and judgment than about knowing that God deeply loves us despite our successes or failures. He loves us no matter what our performance has been. I state this not to give license to sin, but to recognize that the central character trait of God is love, not judgment. God only gave two primary directives in the Old Testament and repeats them in the New Testament: "Love God with all your heart and love your neighbor as yourself."[5] You will fulfill all other things by fulfilling this command. In order for that to be a reality, you must believe you are loved and you must love yourself. You cannot love God or others if you don't believe you are loved and you don't love yourself. We love in response to perceived love. We become vulnerable enough to be loved. Yet from the beginning, humans rejected this in favor of what they perceived to be freedom. This resulted in being separated from the intimacy of our Heavenly Father.

God created us foremost for relationship and second for mission. He desires our companionship. His heart longs to connect with our heart. He reveals this in one of my favorite passages from Jeremiah

9:23-24: Thus says the Lord: "Let not the wise man glory in his wisdom, let not the mighty man glory in his might, nor let the rich man glory in his riches; but let him who glories glory in this, that he understands and knows Me, that I am the Lord, exercising loving-kindness, judgment, and righteousness in the earth. For in these I delight," says the Lord.

The Door to True Intimacy is Often Pain

> *He also brought me out into a broad place; He delivered me because He delighted in me (Ps 18:19).*

Many of us believe we are simply unlovable. The wounds we have received early in life have dictated what we perceive and believe about ourselves and God. When we received these wounds it often resulted in shame and subsequent performance in an effort to gain love from those around us. However, until we are healed we will sabotage relationships subconsciously to prove what we perceive about ourselves–that we are unlovable. It takes others who are close to us to recognize this root issue in our lives and be willing to love us unconditionally. God forces us back to the place of our wound in order to bring us to a place of freedom and deliverance into the broad place He desires for each of us.

Francine Rivers, in her book, *Redeeming Love,* provides a good illustration of this truth. Her fictional book based on the biblical story of Hosea and Gomer is set in the 1800s during the time of cowboys, the gold rush and prostitution. The female character is sold into prostitution early in life due to a mother who chose the same lifestyle because of a difficult childhood. A farmer comes to rescue her from this life against her own will but he has no idea of the challenge it will require for her to overcome her beliefs about herself and to accept his unconditional love for her. She runs away countless times despite his loving care for her. She believes she is unlovable and undeserving of his love so she sabotages their relationship continually to prove that to herself and to him. It is not until she becomes vulnerable enough to accept love–from the farmer and from herself–that she is willing to stay in the relationship. When she begins to receive and experience love, her behavior begins to align with God's ideal. Negative behavior and addictions become non-existent when we begin to believe we are loved. Failure to believe we are loved is the root of most negative behavior.

Revisiting Our Wounds

> *Come, and let us return to the Lord; For He has torn, but He will heal us; He has stricken, but He will bind us up. After two days He will revive us; on the third day He will raise us up, that we may live in His sight. Let us know, Let us pursue the knowledge of the Lord. His going forth is established as the morning; He will come to us like the rain, like the latter and former rain to the earth (Hos 6:1-3).*

God will actually take us into places of very deep pain in order for us to discover true intimacy with Him. The reason this is necessary is that many of us have lived with arrows that have been lodged in our heart for a very long time. We live out our lives from that pain. The wounds caused by these arrows of the soul have prevented us from connecting at a deep heart level with the only person who can remove the arrows and cause healing to take place – our Heavenly Father. Until this happens the enemy of our soul will keep us captive to the pain caused by these wounds. We will hide behind a false self designed to protect us from our true self for fear of exposing our true identity to avoid being rejected. For most of us this is the only path that allows us to move past our superficial, formula-based Christianity. We think we can achieve His presence through a disciplined punch-list of performance-based spiritual activities that often leave us disappointed. Certainly there are things we can do that set the environment for His presence to be realized, but we must be careful not to fall into trying to maneuver God to make something happen as if He were a spiritual vending machine.

God brings us back to the place of our wound in order to learn the truth about our past and become free. When we learn the truth we begin a process of healing. We learn we are not flawed, but were scarred by a person or situation we often had no control over. Do not fear revisiting your past. It can be the door to freedom.

How Men and Women Deal with Pain

Men and women seek to elude the path of pain, rarely understanding that it is actually the doorway to this secret place of intimacy with God. It would seem on the surface the last thing we would want to do. However, unless we visit the source of our pain we will never become healed and free to love and be loved.

During the writing of this book I received a letter from a man who expressed this problem that I would expect is true for many others.

> I've been a Christian for eight years now and find myself still struggling with faith in areas that in my mind I shouldn't be. While I had both parents growing up, my dad was working 70-80 hours a week and if he wasn't too busy to spend time with me, he was too tired. Never having had that bond time with my dad, I know this is an area of struggle for me with God. There is a belief I struggle to break free from, that because my dad was too busy or tired to have time to spend with me, that God is the same way. Also, with not having grown up in a Christian home with parents who knew and loved the Lord, there were grievous mistakes I made that followed me into adulthood. Primarily these were regarding the scripture about honoring our mother and father.
>
> I know God can change and bless my future, but my biggest struggle is with surrender. I've prayed and asked God to help me I don't know how many times, I want to get to that place, but I'm not there and I don't know why it is still such an issue. The other thing is my best friend is a Pastor, he led me to the Lord eight years ago, and more than once I've heard him talk about being

> in love with Jesus. I don't just hear it, I can see it in him. Sadly, though, I want to know what that is like from personal experience, I'm not there. With all of the things I know the Lord has done in my life, even before I was saved, I can't understand why getting to that place with the Lord seems such an insurmountable task for me. I know there are issues of fear, unbelief and other things that tie to both of those. But how do you ever break free from them if you have prayed and asked for help, and still seem to be stuck in the same old place?

My friend above is seeking to deal with unresolved pain in his life that resulted from not experiencing unconditional love during his growing up years. Men and women each seek to avoid pain in different ways. Larry Crabb has summarized these two unique strategies often used to avoid deep pain.

> All of us are trapped by addiction to a desire for something less than God. For many women, that something less is relational control. "I will not be hurt again and I will not let people I love be hurt. I'll see to it that what I fear never happens again." They therefore live in terror of vulnerably presenting themselves to anyone and instead become determined managers of people. Their true femininity remains safely tucked away behind the walls of relational control.

> More common in men is an addiction to non-relational control. "I will experience deep and consuming satisfaction without ever having to relate meaningfully with anyone." They keep things shallow and safe with family and friends and feel driven to experience a joy they never feel, a joy that only deep relating can provide. Their commitment is twofold: to never risk revealing inadequacy by drawing close to people and, without breaking that commitment, to feel powerful and alive. Power in business and illicit sex are favorite strategies for reaching that goal.[6]

Many times we seek to deal with our pain through various forms of addictions designed to resolve the inner pain we feel. All addictions represent a counterfeit desire for genuine love and intimacy. They are isolation chambers created for ourselves designed to mask our pain. Every human being has a desire to be loved. When we do not feel loved we seek to reconcile this emotional pain. So, if you are fighting any kind of addiction – over control of people, sex, drugs, alcohol, workaholism, shopping, overeating—you are seeking to fill a void only God can fill.

I first met Kris at a men's retreat. Kris is an entrepreneur, business owner and public speaker. He travels around the United States speaking in his industry. I found that Kris' story to be like so many marketplace leaders, including myself. Kris had to go through his own journey of discovering the lies, and to revisit his childhood wounds to discover the truth about himself and his relationship to his Father.

> Never before have I known how desperately Satan has tried to hurt and wound me until I became free from bondage after 48 years of slavery. The truth is that it wasn't until I ran out of places to run did I become emotionally and physically fried enough to want to be rescued. In the process of counseling and other men fighting for me I learned about my past including my wound, the message I received from my wounds, the vows and agreements I made, the lies the evil one told me and where I ran from the pain and for validation instead of to the Father. Deep down I was afraid that the Father would punish me and not love me or have time for me. I don't blame my earthly father but Satan sure used my story against me.
>
> I grew up in a very tough family in the city of Detroit where I do not remember my mother or father ever even putting their hand on my shoulder or ever hearing the words "I love you." I barely remember my father or brothers or sister ever even talking to me until I was an adult, so my wound was that ***no words were spoken to me.*** The

message I received from this wound was that ***"you have no value"*** so I ran through life doing whatever I could to create value and prove my worth. The lies were that I had to make it on my own, no one would ever be there for me and the outcome and the results were completely up to me. Satan kept pouring on the lies that there must be something wrong with me and if I ever failed I deserved to be punished. I felt like a small beggar child in life alone and vowed that no matter what I would make it on my own, be self sufficient and never let anyone get too close to me. If they did, they would only hurt me, reject me and I'd be alone and let down. I soon grew into a young man and was not prepared for taking the world on all by myself so I became a "distant, self sufficient man" bent on succeeding no matter what and never knowing what intimacy and true love was.

Little did I know I had become a slave to performance and self sufficiency and with that came a prison. If I could prove my worth and make it on my own all would be well but it was not. I ran to work, money and status for validation and to the woman for comfort. This combination no matter how hard I tried never worked because the only validation I had was when I was working and I actually went through almost a 10 year period of no vacations. If I wasn't working there was no validation, only fear of rejection. When I ran to the woman it only brought shame. I was fried and could no longer strive.

After screaming out at God, "why did you abandon me?" I finally heard his voice. "I have been here all along." I had accepted Christ 12 years earlier but continued to wrestle with trusting Him and trusting that His heart towards me was good. I could only relate to Him as I related to my earthly Father. You're on your own; figure it out with nothing but silence and absence. I told my story at a men's weekend and others mentioned although I grew up in a home, I was literally an orphan. Those words brought tears to my eyes and they prayed over me and I broke agreements with shame and rejection. That night I was awakened from my sleep and heard God say to me, "You are my son, I love you and I'm proud of you." That was the first time I had ever heard those words and ever heard God's voice.

Through friends and the Father's voice I felt the Gospel come alive when I learned that Jesus came to heal my broken heart and set me free. " I was not a slave but a son and if a son then an heir. Jesus continues to show me scripture and show me ***my real identity*** and that is now where I get my validation. He had to take away the places I ran to for validation not to hurt me but for my own good so I could have rest by abiding in him and trusting him as my provider. I wanted that so badly but I was so afraid. I had a good friend mention that "you will never live beyond how you see yourself." That is so true and I had believed a lie. Satan tried to kill, steal and destroy my life and relationships and tried to lie to get me to live from the old broken man who had to earn my worthiness (slave) instead of the new regenerated man (son) with a new identity in Christ. I now know what it means that "ye shall know the truth and the truth shall set you free." I was freed from shame, guilt, bondage, rejection and lots more. The church is awesome but THERE IS MORE and THERE IS LIFE! I never knew the real meaning of Isaiah 61. Jesus came to heal my broken heart and set me free! HE really showed up just for me. The real Isaiah 61 passage is: The spirit of the Sovereign Lord is upon me, because the Lord has "anointed me to preach good news to the poor. He has sent me to bind up the brokenhearted, to proclaim freedom for the captives and release from darkness for the prisoners." I am a son and not a slave and I now know God loves me unconditionally and I no longer have to meet certain standards to feel good about myself.

Men, beware of taking the question of your manhood and the need for love and intimacy to the woman. Our manhood and the need to be loved must come from our relationship with our Heavenly Father. If our Heavenly Father does not become our source of this love we will relate to females in a very unhealthy way. Our wives will either become our "mothers" or they simply become sex objects designed to relieve the pain inside of us. True intimacy between you and your spouse will never become a reality. It can also lead to an addiction. Masturbation and pornography is often the most common pain reliever for men. These are merely symptoms of a greater need to be loved. If you find yourself in an addiction the solution is to confess your sin and begin to accept the love of God. Repent of unbelief that you are not loved by your Heavenly Father. Begin to meditate on scriptures related to the love of God. The scripture says, "The truth shall make you free."[7] This is the starting point toward healing and wholeness.

Disappointment with God

> *Or what man is there among you who, if his son asks for bread, will give him a stone? Or if he asks for a fish, will he give him a serpent? If you then, being evil, know how to give good gifts to your children, how much more will your Father who is in heaven give good things to those who ask Him! (Matthew 7:9-12).*

In order to further understand the unconditional love of God we must understand the heart of God as a Father. During a sabbatical I had a lot of alone time with God. I had hours and hours and hours to reflect on scripture and books that I read. I began to study the nature of God and to confront the disappointment I felt with Him at times. We struggle with His fairness when it comes to evil things that happen in our world. "Is He truly a God of love?" we wonder.

So many of us use the excuse that we cannot love or feel loved by God because of disappointments we have experienced related to God and even our earthly fathers. Jesus must have felt the same sense of deep disappointment when He struggled in the Garden of Gethsemane. His tears over the cross revealed His humanity and his temptation to feel He was being abandoned by His Father. Yet, He knew it was God's will for Him to fulfill His mission to die on the cross. He became one of us on earth and felt the same feelings that you and I feel when we cannot make sense of life and the evil that we think God could change. John the Baptist had the same feelings when he was awaiting death and sent word to Jesus, "Are you really the one or should we be waiting for another?" In essence he was saying, "Surely I would not have to die like this if you are really the Son of God. You wouldn't treat those you love this way." The truth is we are all called to die as part of our commitment to Christ; for most of us this will be for the old man to die spiritually, but for others it will even require a physical death too.[8]

Job concluded God was not love because he attempted to understand his calamities from one viewpoint – his. We are incapable of understanding all the ways of God. Faith requires us to trust that there are things we will not fully comprehend in this lifetime. Job discovered this in the last chapter of Job. "I have heard of You by the hearing of the ear, but now my eye sees You. Therefore I abhor myself, and repent in dust and ashes."[9] He didn't need to understand God; he needed to see God face to face. He needed to understand his issue was with Satan, not God. Satan comes to kill and destroy. God desires to give life and blessing. The problem is we do not understand there is a war in which each of us are participants.

Many believe they must have a reason for their suffering if they are to blindly believe in a God who claims to be love. Without it they believe they cannot reconcile their world with suffering. Not having this resolved leaves many with doubts about a loving God. God has chosen not to address such a question, which leaves us with the decision to trust or not trust without this question being answered satisfactorily. Larry Crabb explains that "As long as our purpose is to have a good time, to have soul-pleasure exceed soul-pain, God becomes merely a means to an end, an object to be used, never a subject rightfully demanding a response, never a love to be enjoyed."[10] God always requires faith as the bottom line to belief and trust. As He so often does, God provides just enough evidence to believe, and just enough evidence to doubt. Only when our faith is shaken do we learn if our faith *can* be shaken. Is there an event that could happen in your life that would make you conclude that God is not love? If so, you may need to become more rooted in His love to avoid having a shaky foundation and to be assured of the Father's love for you.

God set up his own restriction in relating to the humans He created. He decided not to use His power to make them love Him. He knew His creation had to choose to love Him. Free will complicated God's world, but it was absolutely necessary. This would mean He did not act at times the way we think a "loving God" should act. That was a huge risk. Hands off meant He would now be blamed for Satan's activity as His lack of love.

C.S. Lewis, in his classic, *The Screwtape Letters,* creates chief demon Screwtape and depicts him giving advice to his underling, Wormwood. He cites this truth as a law God has established for Himself. "You must have wondered why the Enemy does not make more use of His power to be sensibly present to human souls in any degree He chooses and at any moment. But you now see that the Irresistible and the Indisputable are the two weapons which the very nature of His scheme forbids Him to use. Merely to override a human will (as His felt presence in any but the faintest and most mitigated degree would certainly do) would be for Him useless. He cannot ravish. He can only woo."[11]

The difference between us and Jesus is that Jesus obeyed the Father and chose to believe in the goodness of the Father despite what appearances seemed to communicate. We, too, are faced with the same dilemma. Faith must make a choice sometimes for things that cannot be readily explained. When God gave man free will it complicated things. God chose not to control mankind.

CHAPTER THREE

"You are My Son"

"For you did not receive the spirit of bondage again to fear, but you received the Spirit of adoption by whom we cry out, 'Abba, Father'"(Romans 8:15-16).

We are to live as sons and daughters of our Heavenly Father. And it is important that we know we are sons and daughters.

Twenty years ago a television series was produced called "Lonesome Dove". Set in the 1880s during the time of outlaws and prostitution, it was the story of two Texas rangers, Gus McRae and Woodrow Call, who were best of friends. They decided to leave the town of Lonesome Dove and venture into cattle driving. Newt, a young man who signed on to go with them, was actually Woodrow's son but had no knowledge of who his father was.

Gus reminded his friend often that this boy was his son, but Woodrow would not acknowledge him.

Being from the "old school", a rough and tumble cowboy, Woodrow was a principled man, very private, and not in the habit of expressing his feelings. However, as the movie progressed, he began to show some favoritism to young Newt, indicating their relationship was more than employee to employer. He tried to "give him his name" in his own subtle way. Eventually, Gus told Newt about his father, but Woodrow would never confirm it. Newt desperately desired his father's recognition.

When Woodrow left to bury Gus after his death, he appointed Newt boss of the ranch in spite of his youth and limited experience. It was his way of affirming his son, letting him know he was more than just a cowhand to him. Then when the time came to leave on the trip which would take many months, Woodrow tried to actually say the words that Newt had been waiting to hear from his dad. He looked into the boy's eyes, but could not get the words to come out... he started a syllable, only to stop. He started again, but could not do it. In defeat, Woodrow turned to another cowhand, gave some final instructions, and rode off into the sunset. The cowhand, who was like an uncle to Newt, turned and said in puzzlement, "You know, he spoke to you as though you were kin." Newt, despondent and devastated, responded,

"I don't belong to nobody!" as he rode off with feelings of deep hurt and rejection. Woodrow failed to give Newt the most important things a young man needs from his father—his name, where he comes from, and the words, "I love you". Newt was left to live out his days as an orphan.

The key to experiencing the love of the Father lies in our willingness to live as a son and daughter in trust and vulnerability. And trust and vulnerability are physical fruits of believing that you are loved. If we believe we are loved by the Father, we are able to trust Him. If we do not believe we are loved, we cannot trust or make ourselves vulnerable. Nor can we live under His authority. When this happens we live as slaves and orphans.

You Have a Name in Heaven

> *"He who has an ear, let him hear what the Spirit says to the churches. To him who overcomes I will give some of the hidden manna to eat. And I will give him a white stone, and on the stone a new name written which no one knows except him who receives it" (Revelation 2:17).*

Each of us has a name in Heaven that uniquely fits us. God created you to have a name that represented you and your calling. We all need to know and understand that name. It defines who we are.

God often gave people different names in the Bible when a significant change was about to take place in them to represent God's future plans for them. Abram became *Abraham*. Sarai became *Sarah*. Jacob became *Israel*. Simon became Peter to signify that *Peter* would be a rock Jesus would use to build His church upon.[12]

There is an interesting story behind my name. I was born Omar Smallwood Hillman III. They put the "O" together with the "S" to call me "Os." My grandfather was delivered by Dr. Smallwood. However, no one in my family knows where the name "Omar" came from. It is very strange to have a name like "Omar" growing up in the Deep South in the United States. We have no Muslim roots that I know of.

One day a friend and mentor and I were away on a weekend mountain holiday. We both awoke early that morning and were having coffee when he suddenly looked at me and said, "Do you know the meaning of Omar? You need to know. It has something to do with your future." I was taken by surprise by his abrupt assertion but I had learned to take such times seriously. This was a time of great adversity in my life and I was doing a lot of study and writing about Esau, the brother of Jacob. Esau was a man who despised his birthright for porridge. I was relating Esau to many men and women in the workplace who despised their spiritual birthrights for the pride and greed that can be attained through their marketplace calls at the expense of their spiritual lives. Esau was rejected by God because He failed to recognize the high calling God had upon his life and chose to throw it away on the pleasures of life.

It was 1996 and I had never done any public speaking of any kind. I was trying to recover from a series of personal and business crises in my life. That night I went onto the internet and found the meaning of "Omar." The name has several origins: Arabic for first son and disciple; Hebrew for gifted speaker; German for famous. Omar was the great grandson of Esau.

I was pretty shocked to learn this. Little would I know that years later I would be speaking to many men and women about fulfilling their purpose in life through their vocational calling. I would travel to more than 25 countries, write several books and become an international speaker on the topic of faith and work. As I think about my childhood and young adult years and the idea that I would become a public speaker it seems preposterous to me. I was a shy and reserved person who got so nervous speaking in front of others I could hardly stand up. But God sees our potential and begins the work in us to accomplish it. What I find most interesting is the number of Muslim countries I have been invited to speak in and I continue to get invitations to these nations. I believe God's purpose in giving me this name is yet to be fully understood, but it is clear He is behind giving me this most unusual name.

If we do not receive words of validation and emotional love from our earthly fathers and our Heavenly Father, we will often seek that validation through our achievements like sex, romance novels, shopping, and any number of pleasure-focused activities. We will struggle with uncertainty in our core and will be ruled by fears and the opinions of others, hoping for someone to notice us.

In July 2009 *Time* magazine did a story about the disintegration of marriage in America. One comment of particular interest to me supports this need to know who we are and where we came from. "Children have a primal need to know who they are, to love and be loved by the two people whose physical union brought them here. To lose that connection, that sense of identity, is to experience a wound that no child-support check or fancy school can ever heal."[13]

The name that is written in Heaven about us is God's picture of our soul that is totally unique to us.

It is an affirmation of God's purpose in creating us that is unlike anyone else. He wants to give us a new heart and put a new spirit within us. It is a heart that allows us to express that uniqueness so that we can experience the glory of His creation in us and what we are meant to become. There is no one like you on the earth. You were created totally unique and special to God. Just read God's perspective of His thoughts about you when He created you.

> *For You formed my inward parts; You covered me in my mother's womb. I will praise You, for I am fearfully and wonderfully made; Marvelous are Your works, and that my soul knows very well. My frame was not hidden from You, when I was made in secret, and skillfully wrought in the lowest parts of the earth. Your eyes saw my substance, being yet unformed. And in Your book they all were written, the days fashioned for me, when as yet there were none of them. How precious also are Your thoughts to me, O God! How great is the sum of them! If I should count them, they would be more in number than the sand; When I awake, I am still with You (Ps 139:13-18).*

What name is written on the white stone in Heaven that best expresses the Father's reason for creating you?

CHAPTER FOUR

A Nation in Crisis

Fatherhood is in crisis in America. "Since 1960, the proportion of children who do not live with their own two parents has risen sharply–from 19.4% to 42.3% in the nineties. This change has been caused, first, by large increases in divorce, and more recently, by a big jump in single mothers and cohabiting couples who have children but don't marry. Sixty-five percent of young adults whose parents divorced had poor relationships with their fathers (compared to 29% from non-divorced families)," according to a 2009 study on family life and the importance of marriage released by sixteen of the top scholars.[14] A few years ago I spoke in several cities in South Africa. I asked my host what she thought about the teaching I was giving to the people. I will never forget her words: "It is not teaching they need most; it is a father they need. You represent a spiritual father to them. That is the most important thing you have given them."

When speaking to groups about this message I often conduct an informal survey wherever I speak. I ask the audience this question: "How many of you grew up hearing the words 'I love you' from your earthly father?" No matter where I ask this question the answer is the same. Less than 10% of the audience raises their hands, acknowledging that their fathers said the words, "I love you". Recently I spoke in India. I asked this question among the 225 business leaders who attended my meeting. Less than 5% of the hands were raised.

God, the Father Validated His Son with Words

> *"And suddenly a voice came from heaven, saying 'This is My beloved Son, in whom I am well pleased'" (Matthew 3:17).*

God spoke audibly very few times in the entire Bible. Scripture says God spoke to Moses face to face.[15] The other times were to His Son, at His baptism by John the Baptist, again on the Mount of Transfiguration and again in John 12:26. At two of these events, the Father makes a point to say these words audibly: "For we did not follow cunningly devised fables when we made known to you the power and coming of our Lord Jesus Christ, but were eyewitnesses of His majesty. For He received from God the Father honor and glory when such a voice came to Him from the Excellent Glory: ***'This is My beloved Son in whom I am well pleased.'*** And we heard this voice which came from heaven when we were with Him on the holy mountain."[16]

"I SAW THE LORD WALKING WITH YOU AROUND THE LAKE"

One encounter of personally connecting with the love of the Father came to me through a mentor. This man from another country became a father figure to me. We were talking by phone about a crisis I was experiencing at the time and he stopped midstream in our conversation and said, "Os, you must know something. I love you. I really love you. I believe God has given us a special kind of relationship. I just want you to know that."

I was taken by surprise at his comment and felt unprepared to respond. I said a respectful, "I love you too. You have meant a lot to me." But there was no emotion behind my words because I did not know how to respond. The following day as I was walking around the lake where I go about 3 times a week. My mind went back to the phone call, and I began to weep.

I wept for 30 minutes. The Lord was saying He loved me through my mentor. We often experience sonship personally by the Holy Spirit operating through an earthly father figure when our earthly fathers are no longer around. He reminded me that I had not heard those words from my father, even though I knew he did love me. He simply did not verbalize it. I had not actually thought about this fact until this moment.

> *Come, and let us return to the Lord; for He has torn, but He will heal us; He has stricken, but He will bind us up. After two days He will revive us; on the third day He will raise us up, that we may live in His sight. Let us know, let us pursue the knowledge of the Lord. His going forth is established as the morning; He will come to us like the rain, like the latter and former rain to the earth (Hosea 6:1-3).*

The path to true sonship can be very difficult. I mentioned earlier that God requires us to visit our wound before we can fully experience the love of the Father. He desires to heal those places in our lives in order that we can relate to our Father through intimacy instead of performance. That path can require some extended pain along the way because we must recognize how the pain has affected us and others in our lives.

We must recognize we are in a spiritual war against unseen principalities and powers. Satan wants to destroy our destinies. Such was the case I found myself in during a period of about 2 years. I had become so discouraged with this process that my very faith was being shaken. The enemy made me question whether I even had a ministry anymore. Satan did not want me to gain such freedom. I literally had days where I questioned the existence of God for His lack of answer to my prayers or breakthrough in my situation.

C.S. Lewis once said "There are two mistakes the church makes when dealing with the devil: to blame everything on him or to blame nothing on him."[17] A recent Barna Study found that just one-quarter of adults (27%) are convinced that Satan is a real force. Even a minority of born again adults (40%) adopt that perspective.[18] It's no wonder we have a weak Church. There is a balance we must draw when it comes to being accountable for our dysfunctions and recognizing the spiritual forces behind our issues. It requires a response in both cases.

Satan's attacks came through an accusing spirit against me during this period to discourage me from gaining this freedom. About nine o'clock one evening I received a very hurtful email from someone while I was alone at home. This email was filled with lies and accusations against me. Nevertheless, because it came from someone close to me, it affected me greatly. I was quite distraught over this. However, within five minutes of receiving this email I received a phone call from a friend in Chicago who was leading a prayer group. They had never called me before. "We were praying for you and sensed that you were in need of prayer right at this moment and we wanted to know if we could pray for you." They prayed for me over the phone and shared a scripture verse with me that spoke directly to the content of the email message I had just received. I saw this as the care of my Father in Heaven helping me walk through a difficult situation, letting me know He was with me in the battle and He was bringing me into a new place with Him. We are all in a war in which the enemy of our souls desires to keep us from experiencing the love of our Father.

During this season I often walked at a nearby lake where I cried out to the Lord about the situation I was going through. Frankly, I felt like my prayers were simply hitting a brick wall. I felt nothing. Nevertheless, I kept walking and kept praying out of obedience and blind faith. I often played golf simply to get my mind off of my circumstances. Then, after doing this for more than 18 months I went to my church for prayer with two trusted intercessors. They knew me but did not know what I was walking through. They prayed over me and the Lord revealed many things in that prayer time that confirmed to me that God was in the midst of my struggle and He was there, even though I could not recognize it. Then, one of the intercessors said these words to me: "I heard the Lord say 'it is time for you to have some fun and to relax—to walk around a lake or play golf'—I don't know if you do these things, but I saw you doing these things. I saw the Lord doing these things with you and being with you. During these times I saw the Lord downloading incredible new ideas and a new vision to you. These were times you were not striving to gain insights, but they were relaxed times that the Lord was downloading to you. He is bringing you into a place of being His son."

When I heard these words I began to weep. This woman knew nothing about my walking or playing golf. I walked 3-4 times a week around a lake near me and used that time to pray. However, many days I felt like I was praying to a concrete wall. I felt my prayers were bouncing off the walls. However, here was God speaking directly to me saying, "I have been with you at the lake and even when you play golf." The Lord was personally speaking to me through another person to let me know He was in the midst of the struggle. I was in the midst of writing this book and He truly was teaching me to be His son. They were correct when they said God was giving me new downloads and new vision. I often could see a future that had not materialized and seemed farfetched at the time. Some of these things are yet to be realized, but remain a vision that I believe He has placed in my heart.

I walked away from that prayer session with a renewed hope to continue to walk through my season of adversity and that He really was with me. Satan had tried to convince me God had abandoned me. The Bible tells us that He will never leave us nor forsake us. However, sometimes life can beat you down so badly that it is not enough to read a passage of scripture and force yourself to believe it. You must experience it to believe it. God allowed me to experience it in this situation.

Each of us must ultimately experience the love of the Father, not just know about it. That is when our hearts begin to change.

One Man's Journey to Sonship

Bradley was born with cerebral palsy in South Africa. He barely survived his birth. He did not walk until he was four years old. One leg was longer than the other and he could not speak well. For most of his life, his hands shook and he had little control over them. Feelings of rejection and bitterness at his plight were common occurrences during his growing-up years. During his school years, he was mocked and ridiculed by kids and generally rejected by society.

At age 18, his father was told to take him to a healing service. That night, his leg divinely grew two inches. He no longer walked needing a lift in his orthopedic shoes. Bradley met the Savior and began to grow in his intimacy with Him. Over time God began to heal his cerebral palsy. God began to speak to him and show him things. Prayer became his source of comfort and strength. God gave Bradley insights about people and situations. Today, Bradley travels around the world as an internationally known teacher and founder of Yada, which began as an intercessory school and now is a school to help believers discover their destiny through an intimate journey with the Lord. Literally hundreds of hours of knowledge about the way God speaks to His children have been birthed in and through Bradley, who has become a dear friend and intercessor with our ministry today. However, Bradley struggled to experience the love of his Heavenly Father. Part of this was due to his childhood wounds of rejection and a detached father who he who was a workaholic. Then at age 34 Bradley's father was murdered in South Africa and because of the miraculous way the Father prepared him for this event what could have made him feel abandoned caused him to experience the Father's love in one of the most powerful ways. He now says, "It does not matter what you go through; what matters is how intimate are you with the Father who can carry you through anything."

> I was born and raised in a Christian home. My father was a pastor, but had to leave the ministry, as it could not sustain the family financially. However in his pursuit to be a provider for his family he became a workaholic which was a reason for him eventually losing his family as my mother divorced him.
>
> Growing up I knew he loved me with all his heart, but coming from a stiff upper lip British mindset he never expressed that love to me much through his words or a hug. In 34 years of my life with him I can only remember enjoying 2 vacation times with him. As a result when I got radically saved and started pursuing an intimate relationship with the Lord I found it hard at first to relate to Him as Father as it did not

trigger good emotions in me. This directly affected my prayer life as well. However my point of breakthrough came when I saw that until I loved and accepted myself I would never love God or others correctly.

Once I allowed the love of the Father to heal my rejection and pain from a perceived rejection from my father and a true rejection from my peers due to my battles with cerebral palsy, life radically changed for me. It has been a journey to freedom, not a onetime deliverance session or prayer that has changed my life. As I started the ministry subconsciously I thought I had to always be ministering in order to gain the Father's love and acceptance. This led me to be totally performance-driven and to get a false identity from my ministry instead of from my Father. The Father began putting His finger on this issue and I had some breakthroughs but was still pretty blind to it.

Four nights before my father was murdered a family adopted me into their family, not knowing what would happen four days later. As I talked over becoming a spiritual son to this man he shocked me by saying "I want to relate to who you are not to what you do." That rocked my performance world, but today my life is not the same as I am learning to get my identity from my Father, not my performance, as I am simply being a Father pleaser. All I had heard of about fatherhood prior to this was really about parenting, but I've come to see all we have to do is follow Jesus' model of becoming a son to our Father and model our sonship as Jesus did going from a child to a son to a father.

CHAPTER FIVE

The Father's Love is All Around Us

The earth is full of His loving-kindness (Ps 33: 5).

Experiencing the personal love of God can come in the most unlikely ways. More often than not, it will come through another person or personal circumstance when God says, "I am here and I know you and love you." Just recently my sister Diane told me about an unusual experience she had. A few years ago our mother died in a nursing home at 88 years old. She had dementia for the last several years of her life. Her name was Lillian. My sisters did most of the care and visiting of my mom as I lived 3½ hours away. Mom's decline deeply affected our family and there were many stressful times. Diane had a tumultuous childhood with mom, and as an adult, she struggled with feelings of anger and disappointment. However, during these caretaking years, her heart changed. She genuinely fell in love with mom during that period. Mom's death was particularly hard on Diane because of her feelings of guilt from earlier years. It was also hard because she lost a relationship that had become very special to her that she never had with our mom during her growing up years. Her experience in the nursing home had such an impact on her that after the death of my mom she went to work at a nursing home because she actually loved caring for the elderly.

Recently Diane was caring for a lady in her nursing home named Mrs. Mobley. She loved Mrs. Mobley and described her as having the same temperament, personality and sweetness that my mother exhibited when she cared for her. In fact, Mrs. Mobley's first name was Lillian. Imagine that! It was a gift to be able to care for her. When she passed away, Diane was heartbroken all over again because she reminded her so much of our mother. Then the most amazing thing happened. The obituary revealed something very interesting about Mrs. Mobley. It turns out that Mrs. Mobley had a daughter named... Diane... who had died a few years earlier. When my sister learned this, it was just about all she could handle. What are the chances her name would be Lillian and her daughter's name, Diane?

Could it be that even when God shows us His love and personal involvement in our lives in the most unusual ways, it still requires a level of faith to believe and to embrace that love? In Psalm 33:5 we learn that "The earth is full of His loving-kindness." His love is all around us. It is up to us to recognize His handprints.

CONNECTING EMOTIONALLY WITH GOD AND OTHERS

In order to become an effective friend of God and friend to those we are close to, we must learn to be vulnerable and develop an ability to share feelings from our heart. It is a vital step to becoming a real person with whom others can connect with emotionally. This is not easy to do if your parents did not teach you to share your emotional life with others as was the case with myself. Emotional vulnerability is especially hard for men. Author Dr. Larry Crabb states, "Men who as boys felt neglected by their dads often remain distant from their own children. The sins of fathers are passed on to children, often through the dynamic of self-protection. It hurts to be neglected, and it creates questions about our value to others. So to avoid feeling the sting of further rejection, we refuse to give that part of ourselves we fear might once again be received with indifference. When our approach to life revolves around discipline, commitment, and knowledge [which the Greek influence teaches us] but runs from feeling the hurt of unmet longings that come from a lack of deeper relationships, then our efforts to love will be marked more by required action than by liberating passion. We will be known as reliable, but not involved. Honest friends will report that they enjoy being with us, but have trouble feeling close. Even our best friends (including spouses) will feel guarded around us, a little tense and vaguely distant. It's not uncommon for Christian leaders to have no real friends."[19]

I relate very much to Larry's comment. Although I was raised in a middle-class family that never lacked for anything, me and my four sisters did lack some very important emotional foundations during our growing up years. We were raised in a shame-based environment. Shame can be expressed in subtle and not-so-subtle ways. We were often shamed for crying. There was little physical affection and words of affirmation. This led to performance to make up for the lack of words and physical intimacy. I learned later in life this affected me in my ability to verbalize through words because words were shut down in me early in life. What I thought was a quiet personality was, in fact, a result of a form of rejection that took place in early child-hood. This was not totally my parent's fault as this was passed down generationally to them. We all parent the same way we were parented unless we recognize the negative patterns that may have affected us and become intentional about changing them.

Many of our youth today suffer from emotional abandonment. Their parents have failed to invest emotionally in their children and they grow up angry, not knowing why they are angry. It is because they were not given what every child needs—emotional intimacy with their mothers and fathers. Emotional validation tells them they have value and are loved. Withholding affirming words and appropriate physical affection can be as damaging as negative words or no words.

CHAPTER SIX

It's All about the Heart

> *And because you are sons, God has sent forth the Spirit of His Son into your hearts, crying out, "Abba, Father!" Therefore you are no longer a slave but a son, and if a son, then an heir of God through Christ (Galatians 4:6-7).*

One of the first times we discover that God's heart was hurt is in Genesis: "Then the Lord saw that the wickedness of man was great in the earth, and that every intent of the thoughts of his heart was only evil continually. And the Lord was sorry that He had made man on the earth, and *He was grieved in His heart.*[20] God has deeply held feelings and has a heart and emotions. Sometimes we only think about the omnipotent, all-powerful characteristics of God. Here we see an emotional and passionate God.

God speaks a great deal about the heart. Throughout the scripture we hear Him grieve that the people of Israel did not love Him from their heart—that their hearts were far from Him. We read in scripture about a God who appears to be frustrated with His creation's response to His love. He so desired to be loved by His creation, and yet they spurned Him at every turn. He finally gave up when He destroyed all creation except for Noah and his family. He started over.

He desperately desired that His creation would love Him, but they refused. He tried again and again and finally did the ultimate—He came to earth as a human being in Jesus. God offered a long, extended time of visibly seeing, touching and experiencing the heart of God in Jesus. For the first time we could see what God the Father was like by seeing Him manifested as a human being. "If you had known Me, you would have known My Father also."[21] Jesus reprimanded the Pharisees often because their hearts were far from God. They sought to gain spiritual knowledge and power without knowing the Father. Religion only turns us into performance slaves; relationship with Jesus and our Father makes us sons and daughters.

Jesus came to do only what the Father wanted Him to do on earth. "For I have not spoken on My own authority; but the Father who sent Me gave Me a command, what I should say and what I should speak. And I know that His command is everlasting life. Therefore, whatever I speak, just as the Father has told Me, so I speak."[22] Jesus was the Father's representation on earth. He represented the heart of the Father. When Jesus came to raise Lazarus from the dead it says Jesus wept when He saw him because he was his friend. He was showing the Father's heart for the situation. Jesus healed so many because He was representing the Father's heart to heal the brokenhearted.

Satan Wants to Shut Down Your Heart

> *For though you might have ten thousand instructors in Christ, yet you do not have many fathers; for in Christ Jesus I have begotten you through the gospel (1 Corinthians 4:15-16).*

One of the primary ways Satan wants to destroy your life is to shut down your heart. Jesus revealed the contrast between His plans and Satan's in John 10:10: "The thief does not come except to steal, and to kill, and to destroy. I have come that they may have life, and that they may have it more abundantly." This verse is speaking of false prophets who will come to deceive God's elect. However, in 1 Peter 5:8-9, Peter tells us to "Be sober, be vigilant; because your adversary the devil walks about like a roaring lion, seeking whom he may devour." Satan tried to kill Jesus at birth. "And the dragon stood before the woman who was ready to give birth, to devour her Child as soon as it was born."[23] He tried to kill Moses at birth to prevent him from fulfilling his important destiny to free a nation from slavery and lead them to the Promised Land. Satan literally wanted to kill you at birth. If he couldn't do that he would try to kill your destiny in your childhood. Satan knew that if He could hurt you at the deepest level—at your heart level early in life—he would effectively destroy anything good coming from your life. You would not relate to God, you wouldn't relate to others on a heart level, and you would attempt to live your Christian life based on performance, independence and legalism, never experiencing God at a heart level. He would try to wound you throughout your childhood so that you would be immobilized as an adult, attempting to deal with the effects of your woundedness. Your dysfunction would drive you through your adult life unless something dramatic happened that forced you to address your wound in order to become healed and free of its affects. Satan wants our past to become our future. He wants to steal our Father-created glory that each of us was created to celebrate. Psalms 4:2 says, "Oh ye sons of men, how long will ye turn my glory into shame?" He wants to keep us in the shame of our past.

"YOU HAVE A HOLE IN YOUR HEART"

I sat in the doctor's office when I was about 10 years old and heard the doctor say these words: "You have a hole in your heart." This heart murmur prevented me from playing sports for a while until I finally rebelled and demanded to play regardless of my condition, and mom gave up trying to convince me. Now in my fifties as I write this, I have never had a problem with it, though it did keep me out of the military. However, I am not sure if that was due to the heart murmur or the fact the doctor examining the 300 inductees that day was my Dad's golfing partner every Saturday. I was drafted with the number 74 in the lottery that pretty much insured I would go to Vietnam in 1971.

In some ways those words would be a prophetic declaration of my failure to live from my heart and I would require a heart transplant spiritually. The wounds that would affect my heart would keep me from being able to love God from my heart and love others. Wounds caused by shame, performance, perfectionism, lack of emotional validation through words and affection–all would contribute to my "heart condition". This process was a journey toward wholeness, a healed heart and a new relationship with my Father.

Ask God to help you discover those places in your heart that may still be shut down. Ask Him to lead you into a new place of the heart even if it might require a risk on your part.

CHAPTER SEVEN

Living as Sons and Daughters

> *"I will be a Father to you, and you shall be My sons and daughters," says the Lord Almighty (2 Corinthians 6:18).*

Satan wants us to see ourselves as slaves and orphans, not sons and daughters. The marketplace wants to make us slaves living from performance instead of our heart.

In Luke 15 we find the story of the prodigal son. Jesus tells this story of a son who asked for an early inheritance, then floundered it away through a sinful life. Once he realized his sin, he repented. The father welcomed him back and did not even make mention of his sin. He rejoiced over the return of this son. This is a picture of the unconditional love of our Heavenly Father. His brother, however, was a picture of a son living as a slave. He lived to please the father through his performance. His works made him feel entitled to preference and he was angry with the father's unconditional acceptance of the wayward son. His pride revealed that he was not living as a son, but a slave.

Before we were born again into God's Kingdom we were all slaves and orphans. However, all of us are adopted as sons and daughters when we receive Christ into our lives. "Now I say that the heir, as long as he is a child, does not differ at all from a slave, though he is master of all, but is under guardians and stewards until the time appointed by the father. Even so we, when we were children, were in bondage under the elements of the world. But when the fullness of the time had come, God sent forth His Son, born of a woman, born under the law, to redeem those who were under the law, that we might receive the adoption as sons.

> *And because you are sons, God has sent forth the Spirit of His Son into your hearts, crying out, 'Abba, Father!' Therefore you are no longer a slave but a son, and if a son, then an heir of God through Christ."*[24]

Living as a son is the key to living a victorious Christian life. Joseph lived as a son, not as a slave. His father Jacob doted on him. In fact, his father gave too much favoritism to his son, attracting spirits of envy and jealousy which almost resulted in murder. Even when Joseph was made a slave in Egypt, he still lived as a son. A slave would have become bitter and would have retaliated for his circumstances. However, Joseph entrusted himself to his Father as evidenced by his behavior. He was thrown four difficult tests and he passed each one of them with flying colors. He passed the test of betrayal by forgiving God and his brothers. He passed the sexual temptation by fleeing from Potiphar's wife and going to prison for his righteousness. He passed the perseverance test when he was forgotten after giving a dream interpretation to the cupbearer. And, he passed the stewardship test when he refused to repay all those who had betrayed him and became a faithful steward over the resources of Egypt. Joseph lived 81 years after being elevated from the prison cell. He could never have passed those tests had he not lived as a son. The one thing he always wanted more than anything else was to see his father again. The father-son connection was strong in Joseph and this is why he was successful in his trials.

> *And God sent me before you to preserve posterity for you in the earth, and to save your lives by a great deliverance. So now it was not you who sent me here, but God; and He has made me a father to Pharaoh, and lord of his entire house, and a ruler throughout all the land of Egypt.*[25]

When God delivered Joseph from prison, he took him from prison to the pinnacle of power. Many of us have taught that Joseph was second in command to Pharaoh. Actually, Joseph was over his entire household. He may not have had the title of Pharaoh, but from a spiritual position, Joseph was over the entire nation. However, a closer examination of scripture tells us two very important things about his advancement. The purpose of Joseph's deliverance was "to save the lives of his brothers for the sake of a new nation and for Joseph to "spiritually father Pharaoh." How could it happen that a 30-year old would father someone possibly twice his age? It is because it was a spiritual relationship. Joseph never lost sight of who he was. He never lived as an orphan or a slave. He could be a father to Pharaoh because he was a good son first. He was able to forgive and see a larger story to his life because of his position as a son that he never rejected. This allowed him to operate from an intimate relationship with his Heavenly Father, to have dreams and interpret dreams and to gain super-natural marketplace strategies that would give him favor among the leaders of government because he was a problem solver, not just a religious person. This is also why he did not succumb to the temptations that come with power and influence and wealth. He remained a steward of God's purposes on the earth for the nation of Israel and Egypt. This is why many marketplace leaders cannot be entrusted with wealth and influence today. They still live as orphans and slaves by seeking to achieve value through their accomplishments rooted in performance, workaholism, money and fear of failure.

Joseph lived a life that others were attracted to. His life was rooted in his position as a son of his Heavenly Father and his father Jacob. Joseph's fondness of his father was expressed many times in the scriptures. The one thing he longed for more than anything during those years of separation was to be reunited with his father. This is a picture of the spiritual son to father relationship.

DAVID LIVED AS A SON

> *"The Lord has sought out for Himself a man after His own heart, and the Lord has appointed him as ruler over His people..." (1 Samuel 13:14).*

David is a life of contrasts and contradictions. The Bible says in Psalm 51:5 that David was conceived in sin. It's possible David was an illegitimate son based upon this verse, although we do not have a way of knowing this for sure. This might explain why his father Jesse did not even think of him when Samuel came to select one of his sons to be the next king. This iniquity is also an explanation for the sexual generational sins that surfaced throughout his life. David committed adultery and murder and was an awful father who neglected his children. He had multiple wives when the scripture prohibited polygamy for kings. You could build a case against David that he had a sexual addiction. However, David's experience clearly shows us that obedience and failure is not God's primary criteria for receiving or not receiving His blessing and favor. David was much like the prodigal son. He is mentioned more than any character in the Bible with 62 chapters devoted to him in the Old Testament and 59 references in the New Testament. The one overriding characteristic that God saw in David is that He loved God from his heart. He wrote most of the Psalms and demonstrated a heart that, despite being trampled upon many times, was totally sold out to God. His love relationship with God was an intimate one. David truly related to God as a son. It is clear God became his father because of his understanding of authority. "My son, give me your heart, and let your eyes observe my ways."[26] Many of us fail to live under authority and relate to God as slaves. Saul lived as a slave, not a son.

Jesus lived His life as an earthly son and a Heavenly Son. He related to the Father in every decision He made. He said He never did anything unless the Father led Him to do it. He was on earth to do the will of the Father and to please His Father.[27] His ability to live as a son also allowed Him to be a Father to us while on earth.[28] He was here to give evidence of what the Father was like. "Jesus said to him, 'Have I been with you so long, and yet you have not known Me, Philip? He who has seen Me has seen the Father; so how can you say, "Show us the Father"? 'Do you not believe that I am in the Father, and the Father in Me? The words that I speak to you I do not speak on My own authority; but the Father who dwells in Me does the works. Believe Me that I am in the Father and the Father in Me, or else believe Me for the sake of the works themselves.'"[29] "For I have not spoken on my own authority; but the Father who sent Me gave Me a command, what I should say and what I should speak. And I know that His command is everlasting life. Therefore, whatever I speak, just as the Father has told Me, so I speak."[30] Jesus shows us that a true son is always about doing the will of the Father out of a love motivation and desire to please Him.

On the following pages is a comparison of what it means to live as a son, versus a slave.

Living as a son	*Living as a slave*
And because you are sons, God has sent forth the Spirit of His Son into your hearts, crying out, "Abba, Father!" Therefore you are no longer a slave but a son, and if a son, then an heir of God through Christ. –Gal 4:6-7	Unless the Lord builds the house, They labor in vain who build it; Unless the Lord guards the city, The watchman stays awake in vain. It is vain for you to rise up early, To sit up late, To eat the bread of sorrows; For so He gives His beloved sleep. –Ps 127:1-2
Believes and experiences the unconditional love of the father.	Believes he must perform to gain the father's love.
Experiences sonship as an heir based on his position to the father.	Believes becoming an heir is tied to performance, not his position as a son.
Rests in the security of his father's provision.	Believes provision is only through performance.
When I fail I am still loved.	When I fail I believe I deserve judgment.
I'm a steward of what my father entrust to me.	I am entitled to a share of anything I do.

Living as a son	*Living as a slave*
I love my dad's character. (unconditional love)	I resent my dad's character. (wants conditions)
Value is totally based on position as a son.	Value is only based on what I do and how well I do it.
Love is experienced.	Love is earned.
Receives gracefully.	Expects an entitlement.
Recognizes sins, repentant	Self-righteous, prideful
Lives from the heart	Lives from legalism
Believes he/she is loved	Believes he/she is defective (shame)
Operates in the inner and outer court as both king and priest	Operates only in the outer court of performance as a king
Godly Kingdom lifestyle defined by grace and redemption	Worldly kingdom perspective defined by performance and posturing
Lives under God's authority	Rejects God's authority

GOD DISCIPLINES HIS SONS AND DAUGHTERS

> *If you endure chastening, God deals with you as with sons; for what son is there whom a father does not chasten? But if you are without chastening, of which all have become partakers, then you are illegitimate and not sons. Furthermore, we have had human fathers who corrected us, and we paid them respect. Shall we not much more readily be in subjection to the Father of spirits and live? For they indeed for a few days chastened us as seemed best to them, but He for our profit, that we may be partakers of His holiness (Heb 12:7-11).*

In order to be a legitimate son or daughter we must allow our Father to discipline us at times. Discipline is always for our *profit*. God's desire is that we all become more like His Son, Jesus. That requires "pruning the branch" along the way. And God doesn't prune dead branches, only those that are alive and yielding fruit. This was true of His own Son. "Though He was a Son, yet He learned obedience by the things which He suffered.[31]

CHAPTER EIGHT

Understanding the Role of Our Heavenly Father

"Let us therefore come boldly to the throne of grace that we may obtain mercy and find grace to help in time of need" (Hebrews 4:16).

Jesus, the Holy Spirit and the Father each have a distinct role to play in the Kingdom of God. We are to relate to each in a specific way. One of the most important distinctions is regarding prayer. Our Father is our provider. The root word for father is "source". Whatever needs we have, we are instructed to make our requests known directly to the Father in the name of Jesus. Jesus is our advocate to the Father. Jesus modeled this in the Lord's Prayer. We are to come to our Father boldly, not sheepishly. "Let us therefore come boldly to the throne of grace that we may obtain mercy and find grace to help in time of need."[32]

Do you remember how you related to your earthly father as a child when you wanted ice cream or maybe money to buy something? You asked him boldly, with excitement and anticipation that he was going to give it to you. Why? Because you knew he loved you! The only reason he would not give you what you wanted was if it might not be to your benefit to receive it.

A quick summary provides each of the Trinity member's unique distinctions and roles.

Jesus

- Savior, atonement for sin (John 3:16; 1 John 2:2)
- Have fellowship with the Father and the Son, friendship (John 15:15; 1 John 1:4)
- Intercessor/Advocate to the Father for us (Hebrews 4:14-16; 1 John 2:1)
- To be worshipped (Matthew 2:11)
- Will Judge, the Father judges no one (John 5:22; John 17:5 ; John 8:16)
- Son can do nothing of Himself, but what He sees the Father do (John 5:19-20)
- Jesus is the only way to the Father (John 14.6)
- Restore and reconcile all things (Colossians 1:19-20)
- Light of the world (John 8:12; 12:46)

- Teaches (John 8:28; Acts 1.1)
- Gives His life (John 10:11)

Father

- He created us. "In the beginning God created the heavens and the earth" (Genesis 1:1-2)
- He alone is to be petitioned for our needs. "Give us this day our daily bread..." (Matthew 6:9) "If you then, being evil, know how to give good gifts to your children, how much more will your Father who is in heaven give good things to those who ask Him!" (Matthew 7:11)
- We worship the Father – "Our Father in heaven, hallowed be Your name" (Matthew 6.9; John 7:5)
- The Father extends forgiveness of sin through the blood of Jesus (John 3:16) "And forgive us our debts, as we forgive our debtors. And do not lead us into temptation, but deliver us from the evil one" (Matthew 6:12)
- Have fellowship with the Father and the Son (1 John 1:4)
- He teaches (John 8:28)
- He gave His Son (John 3:16)

Holy Spirit

- He is our teacher—"For the Holy Spirit will teach you in that very hour what you ought to say." – (Luke 12:12)
- He is our helper—"But the Helper, the Holy Spirit, whom the Father will send in My name..." (John 14:26)
- He is our source of power—"But you shall receive power when the Holy Spirit has come upon you..." (Acts 1:8)
- He is our comforter comfort—"And walking in the fear of the Lord and in the comfort of the Holy Spirit, they were multiplied" (Acts 9:31)
- He is the provider of gifts—"God also bearing witness both with signs and wonders, with various miracles, and gifts of the Holy Spirit, according to His own will?" (Hebrews 2:4)
- He convicts of sin—"And when He has come, He will convict the world of sin..." (John 16:8)
- He testifies about Jesus—"the Spirit of truth who proceeds from the Father, He will testify of Me" (John 15:26-27)

CHAPTER NINE

Jesus Interceded as a Son, Not as a Slave

Our Father in heaven, Hallowed be Your name. Your kingdom come. Your will be done on earth as it is in heaven (Matt 6:9-10).

Jesus is our intercessor before His Heavenly Father. The word intercessor comes from the word "to intercede"—to intervene or mediate on behalf of another. It is a higher form of prayer on behalf of others. The highest form of intercession is to be in complete alignment with the Father's will. However, the Father's will on earth is not accomplished just because it is His will. The Father has limited His authority on earth. His will is accomplished only when someone understands the Father's wishes and prays it into existence. This is why people are awakened in the middle of the night to pray for some situation they have no knowledge of. God is asking that person to intercede so that His will can be done in that person's life.

My friend Craig Hill tells a story about flying a commercial jet many years ago and almost ran out of fuel. He was desperate. They landed just in the nick of time. Years later he met his wife who was part of a mission organization at the time he was flying. Each day their team prayed together and would often get led into prayer over situations they had no knowledge of. One day they were led to pray for two men who were in an airplane and needed to land their plane. They saw one older man and a younger man during their prayer time. They saw that both were wearing blue jumpsuits. This was the detail the Lord was showing them in their intercession time. Now, years later, Craig was sharing his war stories with his future wife Jan during their courtship. Jan recalls the time they were led to pray for two men in an airplane. She asked him if one of them was older than the other and if they were wearing blue jumpsuits. It turns out Jan, now his wife, prayed for Craig and his co-pilot that day many years earlier. In essence, his wife saved his life before they ever knew each other.

Jesus Lived to Please the Father

> *Then Jesus said to them, "When you lift up the Son of Man, then you will know that I am He, and that I do nothing of Myself; but as My Fa-*

> *ther taught Me, I speak these things. And He who sent Me is with Me. The Father has not left Me alone, for I always do those things that please Him." As He spoke these words, many believed in Him (John 8:28-30).*

When Jesus taught the disciples to pray the Lord's Prayer to come into alignment with the Father's will. The Father's will is for Heaven to be represented on earth through His representatives. A son understands the father's wishes and seeks to make it happen because he loves his father and wants to please him. A slave seeks to meet an obligation or use someone to accomplish his own personal agenda. When we pray out of our own will, we are praying in our name. We are praying as a slave. Intercession involves discovering the mind of the Father on a matter and agreeing in prayer that it will happen by faith. We use the authority that the Father has provided to us through the death and resurrection of Jesus Christ. Jesus said that all authority has been given to Him and He gave it to us to represent and enforce the Father's will on earth. Jesus came to destroy the works of the enemy. When He left earth, we were now His representatives to carry on that mission of destroying the works of the enemy on earth. We are to stand in the gap to replace unrighteousness with righteousness on the earth.

Most Christians I encounter really do not understand the basic war that we are engaged in and our responsibility to counter Satan's attacks. When Adam and Eve relinquished their dominion over planet earth to Satan as a result of sin, Satan was entitled to take dominion because of man's sin. Satan's nature is to kill and destroy. When Jesus came to earth He came to reclaim all that was lost according to Luke 19:10. That included dominion over the earth, Satan and his minions. However, just because we have authority does not mean we are going to prevent Satan from having influence on the earth. Man's influence was only effective if we exercised our authority to manifest God's covenant wishes on earth through intercessory prayer. I may have authority over my home, but it does not prevent a burglar from entering my home if he chooses to find a way in. The fact that I don't want him to come into my house is a futile defense unless I create an intentional wall of protection against him. We see a lot of evil in the world today because Satan is left unhindered due to a prayerless Church. God has chosen to exercise His authority only through his representatives manifesting His will through their intercession.

The Holy Spirit is to help us by instructing us on what to pray. Paul tells us in Romans, "In the same way, the Spirit also helps our weaknesses, for we don't know how to pray as we ought. But the Spirit himself makes intercession for us with groanings which can't be uttered. He who searches the hearts knows what is on the Spirit's mind, because He makes intercession for the saints according to God."[33] Jesus is our high priest and intercessor before the Father to enforce His covenants when we pray.[34]

What covenant promise do you need to enforce on earth? Spend time asking the Father what is on His heart He wants you to pray about. This is what it means to pray as a son or daughter.

CHAPTER TEN

Why Restoring the Father-Child Relationship is Key to Our Future

Behold, I will send you Elijah the prophet before the coming of the great and dreadful day of the Lord. And he will turn the hearts of the fathers to the children, and the hearts of the children to their fathers, lest I come and strike the earth with a curse (Malachi 4:5-6).

The last book of the Old Testament is the book of Malachi. This was the last book written before the New Testament writings. There were four hundred years of silence from God between the two Testaments. Scholars believe this silence was due to the nation of Israel living as illegitimate sons and daughters. The last few verses written in Malachi are important to our understanding of what it means to live as sons and daughters and the need to restore a right relationship between fathers and their children.

There are two important events referred to in the above mentioned verse. First, God is telling us that before Jesus would come to earth the first time there would be someone who would announce and prepare the way for Him to come. That person was John the Baptist who came in the spirit of Elijah. That was the coming of the "great day". There is also a "dreadful day" spoken of in the same sentence. Some believe these are two different days and times. The second day would be the return of the Messiah. The second messenger mentioned in Malachi 3 is the messenger of the covenant and speaks of judgment versus redemption.

I have a grown daughter who works in our ministry. She is a product of divorce because her mother and I split up in the 90s. We divorced because I failed as a husband to love and cherish my wife as Christ loved His bride. I failed to love my daughter emotionally during her growing up years. She had emotional scars as a result as she got older. This was due to my own wounds as a child from the loss of my father at age 14 and the lack of emotional validation and shame that I experienced as a child that was not healed until later in life. It was not until much later in life that I understood the affects of my inability to love my daughter and others at an emotional level. These wounds bled into my daughter and my first and even second spouse. As I have become increasingly healed of these wounds, I have been able to reconnect and revisit those places where I had failed as a result of not recognizing these issues. I took responsibility for my failures and hurts I caused once I understood them and the impact they had. This has allowed healing to come to my daughter and our relationship. This is what is needed from fathers in families around the world.

I was an emotionally detached father to my daughter when she was a child. It was not my intent, but I simply modeled what I was taught from my parents and lived from some of my early wounds. God has been gracious to me and my daughter, Charis, to be able to walk through several years of healing between us and be able to openly discuss them. God has turned the father's heart to the daughter's, and the daughter's to the father's.

I've asked her to share a little of her journey with you. Her story takes place during her growing up years when I owned an ad agency in the 80's and early 90's, but also more recently, as I have come to better understand my own fatherhood issues and able to share them with her and take responsibility for my shortcomings. She is now in her late twenties at the time of this writing and works in our ministry.

All throughout my life I felt I was different. When I was around other people, I had this deep sense that there was something wrong with me. It wasn't until just recently that I realized some of the reasons why. These largely related to not being loved emotionally by my dad during my growing up years. Much of my life had been spent in depression, trying to earn love, but then I realized I had no capacity to earn it. "Only if I am perfect can I be loved," I thought. Why did I think this way? Was I somehow intrinsically damaged beyond the ability to be worthy of love? My problem was I thought "being loved" had to do with my performance.

For much of my early years I felt a void. There are still areas I am revisiting to get a clearer understanding of my past in order to gain greater healing today. Mom and dad fought a lot during my childhood. Dad was away on business trips much of the time, and sometimes that was better. At first I really wanted him to come home, but after about 6 or 7 years of age I realized it was probably better if he stayed away. The fighting wouldn't resume if he wasn't there.

Mom was a cute lady, blonde hair, blue eyes, creative, but fiery. I guess I have some of that Sicilian blood in me too. I don't remember seeing my parents showing affection. I always wondered why I didn't see dad show love to my mom. I found myself having anger from this and hating the role she played as a wife and mother, and vowed never to put myself in the same position. He compared her to other women. He was critical of her, and didn't value her opinion. He didn't compliment her or trust her. They didn't seem like friends. Eventually, she began stealing money from him to make a point that her opinion mattered. There wasn't much warmth going on in our home at the time. My mom tried to decorate with lots of hearts to fill the void for the love that wasn't there. The atmosphere felt sterile and cold.

I asked Jesus to come into my heart when I was six. As a young child, I struggled with being overweight, and had nightmares at night. Both of these things worsened the belief that there was something wrong with me, and that I was not lovable. Many children have nightmares at a young age, but I continued to have them until I was about 9. When I think back on those times I think how much two parents fighting really does affect a child. The child doesn't yet have the chemicals in their brain to process it and often take on the guilt of their parent's unhappiness. And when the parents aren't unified this breaks the love bond over the home. Being so young, I remember all I could do was cry. I thought I was the one to blame for all of the fighting. I felt at a loss because I didn't know how to fix it. But a child is never supposed to fix their parent's adult problems.

When mom and dad divorced when I was 12 I remember feeling relieved. Now mom and dad couldn't yell anymore, and they wouldn't be fighting. What I perceived as "the family war" was over. I took on a lot of my mom's burdens because I saw my identity in her. I swore against getting married because I thought, "If that's what marriage is like, I don't want anything to do with it." It had so pained my heart to see them so unhappy for so many years. But, I still had a void in my life from my dad's emotional absence in my life.

A girl is supposed to understand her worth, her value, and her identity from the age of 12 until 17 or 18. Her father is the primary parent to impart identity to the daughter. By this time I had learned to shut off my heart from all men, because anything coming from my earthly father was either an angry remark for my mom, or a complete lack of communication. Although I did not know it at the time, my dad's inability to emotionally and physically love me with hugs had its affect on me. I have learned that the lack of words can bring even more damage than negative words. I concluded that, "I must not be worth anything." The messages I subconsciously absorbed from all of this were that I was unlovable, ugly, unworthy, and different. I felt that I was marked "unacceptable". I felt unworthy of anyone's true acceptance and love, unless I somehow worked to earn it. I gained my acceptance through doing well in school and in trying to be a good person.

At the end of my junior year of high school I decided to go to college early. I was sick of school and was really depressed. That summer, my mom took me out to dinner for my birthday. On the way there I remember feeling so disappointed, so discouraged - I felt I had no purpose for my life. Much of this I learned later was due to the fact that I hadn't felt my fathers' love growing up. I was literally considering suicide while we were driving in the car, but I remember wondering how my mom would survive without me. I remember asking God why was I here? I felt I had no purpose. I tried to hide my tears by looking out the window.

As we drove up to the restaurant though, I saw something that surprised me. A big beautiful rainbow was right above the restaurant. This probably doesn't mean much for most people, but for me, when I saw it, I began to sob. My mom asked me what was wrong, and I couldn't speak through my tears. All throughout my growing up years I loved rainbows. They were my favorite things. And when I saw that rainbow right over the restaurant that day it opened my heart again in hope, and God said, "I love you. This was my first real connection to my Heavenly Father. I felt He said, "This is my birthday present to you. I have a purpose and a plan for your life. And I want to be with you. You *are* worthy of My love." That was the day I rededicated my life to Him, and trusted Him as my Heavenly Father. I was 17 years old.

TURNING THE HEARTS OF THE FATHERS TO THEIR CHILDREN

He will turn the hearts of the fathers to their children, and the hearts of the children to their fathers; or else I will come and strike the land with a curse (Malachi 4:6).

I find it interesting that the scripture above has a progression: *Turn the hearts of the fathers to their children, and the hearts of the children to their fathers.* To me, several things come to mind. 1. The word "heart" involves a connection of mind and emotion to concern one's self with something or someone. 2. The fathers are the head of the household, and are the ones *initiating* these actions, and 3. Scripture says the heart must *receive* love first before it can give it. And we cannot love others if we do not love ourselves.

I think turning the hearts of the fathers to the children has so much to do with personal healing and the corporate healing of families. In Isaiah 61:1 it says, "He has sent me to bind up the brokenhearted, to proclaim freedom for the captives and release from darkness for the prisoners..." God is all about restoring hearts. Our heart is the mechanism by which we are called to serve Him.

God led me back to Him, as Father God, long before I had a restored relationship with my earthly father. However, like my dad shares in this book, I, too, had to revisit my early wounds to allow my Heavenly Father to heal me. It has been painful at times, but very worth it. At the time, my earthly father didn't know how to relate to me, and I didn't know how to relate to him. His black and white views on things pushed me further and further away from him and from any love he was trying to get across. But because of everything that happened before, I didn't see it as love. My response was to hide behind my self-assuredness to avoid being hurt again. I only saw his input as correction - as "You're not right." For me, this was devastating. I thought the only way to be loved was to be right. I wasn't a bad kid, but because he really didn't *know* me, he didn't really know what to say that would speak to me. I had to let go of that relationship for a season so that God could do His healing work in my heart, BEFORE I could have any real connection to my earthly father. I had to understand my Heavenly Father's ability to connect to me at a heart level, something I desperately needed. I had to learn HIS provision, and HIS authority. I had to learn to trust Him. That was especially hard, because I had learned to take care of myself. But progressively, as I gave Him more and more of my heart, I began to get more and more revelations of His love.

Family Changes, Personal Changes

I have seen many changes in my dad over the past several years...and I can see his heart being healed and opened more and more. It's so great to see him be able to relate on a heart level and not be afraid of it, and we have been better able to understand one another. He has been through some very difficult things over the past few years, but has taken them on with so much grace and

> humility. It makes me so proud of him. I know that God will multiply whatever has been deposited in these times of testing and heart rebirth he has undergone during this season of his life. I am grateful to God for showing me how He is my perfect Heavenly Father. I am also so grateful for my dad's courage to recognize and repent for his shortcomings during my childhood as a result of his Heavenly Father working in his life, *so I can have healing in my own.*
>
> Today I have also met someone very special and learned that love is not about my performance, or my perfection. I am in a healthier place emotionally to be able to give and receive love. I have learned that love is just that - about simply giving and receiving, but now it is unencumbered by the baggage or hurts of my past. It is so refreshing to understand God's character through those who understand His true nature. I am excited to move toward the future without being afraid of trying new things and being the successful entrepreneur I know God has called me to be!

Today's generation, like never before, needs spiritual fathers, not just teachers. Malachi says before the 400 years of silence as the very last statement that He desires the hearts of the fathers were to be reconciled to the hearts of the children. If this does not happen, God will strike the earth with a curse. Have we not seen the effects of fatherlessness in our nation? Our marketplaces are being led by men and women who were fatherless and operate from greed and mammon because they know not how to reconcile the fatherlessness in their own lives. The father wound must be healed if we are going to see families and even the marketplaces have a restored Kingdom influence.

There are two important statements found in the second verse of Malachi. First, the Messiah will turn the hearts of the fathers to the children and second, He'll turn the children is hearts back to their fathers before His return. Unless this happens there will be a curse upon the earth. This is a promise of restoration of fatherhood, something we have dearly lost in our generation. This restoration will pave the way for Jesus' second coming, the "great day".

If you are a father, let me encourage you to invest in your children. Validate them as a son or daughter. Use words of encouragement and love so they know without a doubt you love them unconditionally. If there have been breaches in the past, take the initiative as their father to rebuild the relationship. Your children need this, and so do you.

SEPARATED FROM HIS LOVE?

> *For this reason I bow my knees to the Father of our Lord Jesus Christ, from whom the whole family in heaven and earth is named, that He would grant you, according to the riches of His glory, to be strengthened with might through His Spirit in the inner man, that Christ may dwell in your hearts through faith; that you, being rooted and grounded in love, may be able to comprehend with all the saints what is the width and length and depth and height – to know the love of Christ which passes knowledge; that you may be filled with all the fullness of God (Ephesians 3:14-19).*

Do you believe you are loved by God? That was our opening question. The Bible says there is nothing that separates us from His love. "But what about... ?" you may still want to say. Sometimes love requires a high level of faith and trust to keep on believing in spite of our unresolved questions and circumstances. Jesus is the most tangible expression of love we have that reveals the nature and heart of the Father and His willingness to suffer on our behalf. He came and died to help resolve, to some degree, the unresolved questions, realizing for some, even this would not be enough.

Jesus said to him, "'You shall love the Lord your God with all your heart, with all your soul, and with all your mind.' This is the first and great commandment. And the second is like it: 'You shall love your neighbor as yourself.' On these two commandments hang all the Law and the Prophets."[35]

Sons and daughters, let me encourage you to accept your position as a son or daughter of our Heavenly Father. Renounce any sins of believing you have been rejected. God loves you unconditionally as His son or daughter. "And because you are sons, God has sent forth the Spirit of His Son into your hearts, crying out, 'Abba, Father!' Therefore you are no longer a slave but a son, and if a son, then an heir of God through Christ."[36] Each of us must come out of slavery into sonship.

> *For you are the temple of the living God. As God has said: "I will dwell in them and walk among them. I will be their God, and they shall be my people. Therefore come out from among them and be separate," says the Lord. "Do not touch what is unclean, and I will receive you. I will be a Father to you, and you shall be my sons and daughters," says the Lord Almighty. (2 Cor 6:16-18).*

PRAY THIS PRAYER WITH ME

Heavenly Father, I thank you that I am your son, your daughter. I ask forgiveness for not believing your love for me. I renounce any sins of rejection and doubt and unbelief I have harbored in my life. Today I will fully receive your love and begin to walk with you as my Father, in Jesus' name.

Scriptures on the Love of the Father to Meditate On

In addition to meditating on these scriptures, I recommend reading one chapter of John every day for six months. You will learn from Jesus what it means to live as a son.

2 Corinthians 6:18

"I will be a Father to you, and you shall be My sons and daughters," says the Lord Almighty.

Zephaniah 3:17

The Lord your God in your midst, The Mighty One, will save; He will rejoice over you with gladness, He will quiet you with His love, He will rejoice over you with singing.

Psalm 68:5

A father of the fatherless, a defender of widows, Is God in His holy habitation.

Psalm 27:10

When my father and my mother forsake me, then the Lord will take care of me.

Romans 8:15-16

For you did not receive the spirit of bondage again to fear, but you received the Spirit of adoption by whom we cry out, "Abba, Father."

Galatians 4:6-7

And because you are sons, God has sent forth the Spirit of His Son into your hearts, crying out, "Abba, Father!" Therefore you are no longer a slave but a son, and if a son, then an heir of God through Christ.

Matthew 7:9-12

Or what man is there among you who, if his son asks for bread, will give him a stone? Or if he asks for a fish, will he give him a serpent? If you then, being evil, know how to give good gifts to your children, how much more will your Father who is in heaven give good things to those who ask Him!

Matthew 6:26-27

Look at the birds of the air, for they neither sow nor reap nor gather into barns; yet your heavenly Father feeds them. Are you not of more value than they? Which of you by worrying can add one cubit to his stature?

1 Corinthians 4:15-16

For though you might have ten thousand instructors in Christ, yet you do not have many fathers; for in Christ Jesus I have begotten you through the gospel.

John 8:19b

If you had known Me, you would have known My Father also.

John 14:10-11

Do you not believe that I am in the Father, and the Father in Me? The words that I speak to you I do not speak on My own authority; but the Father who dwells in Me does the works. Believe Me that I am in the Father and the Father in Me, or else believe Me for the sake of the works themselves.

John 14:21

He who has My commandments and keeps them, it is he who loves Me. And he who loves Me will be loved by My Father, and I will love him and manifest Myself to him.

John 10:17-18

Therefore My Father loves Me, because I lay down My life that I may take it again. No one takes it from Me, but I lay it down of Myself. I have power to lay it down, and I have power to take it again. This command I have received from My Father.

John 14:23-24

Jesus answered and said to him, "If anyone loves Me, he will keep My word; and My Father will love him, and We will come to him and make Our home with him. He who does not love Me does not keep My words; and the word which you hear is not Mine but the Father's who sent Me.

2 Corinthians 6:18

"I will be a Father to you, and you shall be My sons and daughters," says the Lord Almighty.

Proverbs 23:26

My son, give me your heart, and let your eyes observe my ways.

2 Timothy 1:2

To Timothy, a beloved son: Grace, mercy, and peace from God the Father and Christ Jesus our Lord.

Isaiah 61:1-3

The Spirit of the Lord God is upon Me, because the Lord has anointed Me to preach good tidings to the poor; He has sent Me to heal the brokenhearted, to proclaim liberty to the captives, and the opening of the prison to those who are bound; To proclaim the acceptable year of the Lord, and the day of vengeance of our God; To comfort all who mourn, to console those who mourn in Zion, to give them beauty for ashes, the oil of joy for mourning, the garment of praise for the spirit of heaviness; That they may be called trees of righteousness, the planting of the Lord, that He may be glorified.

Psalm 10:14

But You have seen, for You observe trouble and grief, to repay it by Your hand. The helpless commits himself to You; You are the helper of the fatherless.

Malachi 4:5-6

Behold, I will send you Elijah the prophet before the coming of the great and dreadful day of the Lord. And he will turn the hearts of the fathers to the children, and the hearts of the children to their fathers, lest I come and strike the earth with a curse.

James 1:17

Every good and perfect gift is from above, coming down from the Father of the heavenly lights, who does not change like shifting shadows.

1 John 3:1

How great is the love the Father has lavished on us, that we should be called children of God! And that is what we are!

John 12:49-50

"For I have not spoken on My own authority; but the Father who sent Me gave Me a command, what I should say and what I should speak. And I know that His command is everlasting life. Therefore, whatever I speak, just as the Father has told Me, so I speak."

Rom 8:37-39

Yet in all these things we are more than conquerors through Him who loved us. For I am persuaded that neither death nor life, nor angels nor principalities nor powers, nor things present nor things to come, nor height nor depth, nor any other created thing, shall be able to separate us from the love of God which is in Christ Jesus our Lord.

Eph 3:14-19

For this reason I bow my knees to the Father of our Lord Jesus Christ, from whom the whole family in heaven and earth is named, that He would grant you, according to the riches of His glory, to be strengthened with might through His Spirit in the inner man, that Christ may dwell in your hearts through faith; that you, being rooted and grounded in love, may be able to comprehend with all the saints what is the width and length and depth and height – to know the love of Christ which passes knowledge; that you may be filled with all the fullness of God.

James 1:17-18

Every good gift and every perfect gift is from above, and comes down from the Father of lights, with whom there is no variation or shadow of turning.

Endnotes

1. Psalm 139:17

2 Mike and Sue Dowgiewicz, *Demolishing Strongholds*, Restoration Ministries, Colorado Springs, CO p.10

3. Hebrews 2:12

4. Genesis 4:4-7

5. Deuteronomy 6:4-7

6. Larry Crabb, *Shattered Dreams*, Waterbrook Press, Colorado Springs, CO 2001, p.95

7. John 8:32

8. Galatians 2:20

9. Job 42:5-6

10. Larry Crabb, *Shattered Dreams*, Waterbrook Press, Colorado Springs, CO 2001, p.32

11. C. S. Lewis, *The Screwtape Letters*, Harper Collins, San Francisco, CA 1942, p.39

12. Matthew 16:18

13. http://www.time.com/time/nation/article/0,8599,1908243-3,00.html

14. *Why Marriage Matters*, Second Edition: Twenty-Six Conclusions from the Social Sciences, Institute for American Values, 1841 Broadway, Suite 211, New York, NY 10023

15. Exodus 33:11; Matthew 3:17
16. 2 Peter 1:16-18
17. C. S. Lewis, *The Screwtape Letters,* Harper Collins, San Francisco, CA 1942, p.IX
18. This report draws information from four nationwide telephone interviews conducted by The Barna Group, each inclucing between 1,002 to 1,005 adults randomly selected in 2008
19. Larry Crabb, *Inside* Out, Colorado Springs, Colorado: Navpress, 98-99
20. Genesis 6:5-7
21. John 8:19b
22. John 12:49-50
23. Revelation 12:4
24. Galatians 4:1-7
25. Genesis 45:7-8
26. Proverbs 23:26
27. John 8:29
28. 1 Corinthians 4:14,15
29. John 14:9-11
30. John 12:49-50
31. Hebrews 5:8-9
32. Hebrews 4:16

33. Romans 8:26, 27

34. Isaiah 53:12b

35. Matthew 22:37-40

36. Galatians 4:6-7

ADDITIONAL RESOURCES BY OS HILLMAN

"This book is a home run!"
–*C. Peter Wagner,*
Wagner Leadership Institute

"...extremely practical and genuinely profound ... a must read for all Christians."
–*Ed Silvoso,*
Harvest Evangelism

Os Hillman is one of the leading authorities on faith at work today. *The 9 To 5 Window: How Faith Can Transform The Workplace,* provides an in-depth look at this new move of God and how Christians can practically implement their faith with their work life. Topics include facts on the current movement, how to bring the presence of God into your workplace, developing an intercessory prayer team at work, transforming your workplace, city, and nation for Christ, and much more. Hillman combines his ten years of experience working in the faith at work movement with 20 years as an advertising executive.

Bonus Feature: Includes a Bible study guide at the end of the book, ideal for small groups!

Additional Resources by Os Hillman

"A friend gave me *Upside to Adversity* after I lost my job of 30 years. I thank the Lord for Os' insight and it has renewed my fellowship and love for the Lord."
–*Dan* in Buford, GA

It can be extremely difficult to see God's Hand in our lives when we are going through hardship and adversity. *TGIF Today God Is First Daily Devotional* author Os Hillman knows this all to well. He lost his marriage, his business, and his financial "nest egg" all within a short period of time. Through a challenging seven-year process, Os learned that God was at work using these painful circumstances to prepare him for the calling God had on his life.

If you are in the middle of adversity, or you know someone who is, or just want to learn more about why God allows adversity into our lives, this book by Os Hillman will be a tremendous encouragement as well as a Biblically-grounded discovery of what God may just be up to "behind the scenes" during this painful and challenging time. Hardback, 208pp

ADDITIONAL RESOURCES BY OS HILLMAN

"TGIF has been a daily inspirational and transformational tool for many years now that God has used in my life particularly with the scriptural application in a workplace context."

–*Steve Hyland,*
VP of Retail Merchandising, Coca-Cola North America

In 2000, the first edition of *TGIF Today God Is First* was introduced by Os Hillman, an Atlanta businessman who began writing a daily email devotional with specific application of Scripture to one's work life. TGIF has now become the most popular devotional available on applying your faith in your work life, with over with hundreds of thousands of daily subscribers worldwide.

Volume 2 contains all new 365 daily messages at your fingertips in an attractive hardcover version ready to encourage you daily at work. New messages on topics such as work as ministry, handling disappointments, adversity, integrity, finances, decision-making, hearing God, and much more.

Additional Resources by Os Hillman

TODAY GOD IS FIRST
DAILY WORKPLACE INSPIRATION BY OS HILLMAN

FREE Email Devotional

Start your day by reading an email that encourages you to experience the Lord's presence at work. *TGIF Today God Is First* is a free daily email subscription which has a scripture verse and brief devotional applied to a workplace situation. Subscribe by going to www.marketplaceleaders.org

Marketplace Mentor
by Os Hillman

Marketplace Mentor

Twice a month, receive more in-depth Biblical teaching on various topics related to your work-place calling, marketplace tips, proven business principles, and free and discounted resources via this email e-Zine. *When you subscribe you'll receive three free ebooks by Os Hillman.*

TGIF Today God Is First

365 Meditations on the Principles of Christ in the Workplace. The daily email devotional in book form! *Today God Is First* provides daily meditations that will help you focus your priority on knowing Jesus more intimately every day. Hardback, 400 pp.

Additional Resources by Os Hillman

TGIF Paperback

180 devotionals presented by topics that range from God's will for your life to adversity. The smaller size and weight allows you to carry it with you wherever you go. Paperback, 286 pp.

TGIF Small Group Bible Study

The popular *TGIF Today God Is First* book is now a 12-week, small group Bible study that is ideal for workplace groups. This study includes discussion questions; a work-place application with added scriptures that will allow the leader to extend or reduce the study time. Booklet, 48 pp.

Faith & Work: Do They Mix?

When you have an intimate relationship with Jesus, you will understand that your faith and work are not separate in God's eyes. This book will help you understand why your work IS your ministry. Paperback, 128 pp.

Some products are not available in stores. See one of our websites to order: www.marketplaceleaders.org *or* www.faithandworkresources.com

Additional Resources by Os Hillman

Making Godly Decisions

How can you know if you are making a decision that will be blessed by God? In Making Godly Decisions, you will learn the principles for making good decisions that are also godly decisions. Paperback, 80 pp.

The Purposes of Money

Why does God prosper some, while others still live in need? Can we trust God to provide when we don't have enough? In this book you will discover five fallacies of belief that most people live by regarding money. You will also learn the five primary reasons God gives us money. Paperback, 80 pp.

The 9 to 5 Window Workshop

One day workshop, 6 audio tapes & workbook or our CD Video. This is Os Hillman's complete one-day workshop that helps men and women discover their purpose in work and life. It is loaded with practical application principles to understand God's method of calling, biblical decision-making, and the role adversity plays in every believers life.

ADDITIONAL RESOURCES BY OS HILLMAN

Are You a Biblical Worker?

Here's a self-assessment tool to help you discover where you are in your biblical knowledge of applying faith in your workplace. The inventory test features 50 True/False/Sometimes questions and answers. You will be challenged to think through workplace situations that most of us face every day. Also available as an online electronic test. Great for small group Bible studies.

The Faith@Work Movement

Is there a real move of God in the workplace? If so, what do pastors and church leaders need to know? How can the church mobilize workplace believers to impact their city and nation? The Faith @Work Movement by Os Hillman will answer these and many more questions about the modern-day faith at work movement. Foreword by Dr. Peter Wagner. Paperback, 128 pp.

FaithandWorkResources.com

Faith and Work RESOURCES.COM
"Equipping You to Live Out Your Faith at Work"

Our resources site allows you to find the best in faith and work resources including books and CD messages. Plus you have access to programs such as the Affiliate Partnership which provides you with your own affiliate resource site—allowing you to earn income from your web site. www.faithandworkresources.com

Visit Our Websites

- ☛ *www.MarketplaceLeaders.org*
- ☛ *www.Reclaim7Mountains.com*
- ☛ *www.FaithandWorkResources.com*
- ☛ *www.UpsideofAdversity.com*
- ☛ *www.ICWM.net*

NOTES

NOTES

Notes